[Starting Over]

How to rebuild your best life after heartache

By Ms Kay Spencer

"The women who I love and admire for their strength and grace did not get that way because shit worked out. They got that way because shit went wrong and they handled it. They handled it in a thousand different ways on a thousand different days, but they handled it. Those women are my superheroes."

Elizabeth Gilbert (Author of Eat, Pray, Love)

To my Mum and my brother: *I am incredibly thankful for our small, but mighty unit. On the toughest days you are right by my side, holding me up - I never would have gotten through those days without you. Thank you for constantly having my back and telling me exactly how it is – you are a great source of my motivation and inspiration.*

To my family: *Thank you for your love and support through the hard days. There were times I felt I would never laugh again, but the many ridiculous and incredible moments we have shared has brought great laughter and memories I hope I never forget. You have all contributed to my growth and inspire me in so many ways you cannot imagine – I am truly blessed to be surrounded by such excellence.*

To my readers: *I hope the story of my lowest point reminds you that you have more strength than you know, you are not alone in dealing with heartache and you WILL get through it.*

This is my experience of getting through a difficult period in my life. I am not a therapist, I am not a professional, but I now have experience in dealing with the challenges of trying to put your life back together after a traumatic relationship breakdown. It might help you consider how you can deal with your situation, it might not, but overall, I hope it helps you find comfort in knowing that life is a journey and things will get better. You are not the first person to deal with heartache and you definitely will not be the last, but when you are going through it, you can feel very alone. Remember you are not alone and there is always support available to you.

Contents

Self-care – Rebuilding and focusing on you

Glimpsing back, whilst moving forward

Prologue

In my early 20s I thought my life was completely set. I was in a serious relationship with a guy that I had been dating a few years, who I loved and adored, and we were planning to get married and start a family. I had a job in the city working for a reputable, well known company, in a beautiful, shiny, glass office. Although my role was challenging I enjoyed it and could see an opportunity to climb the ladder to make a good career for myself. My social life was buzzing, I would spend many nights laughing and gossiping with various groups of friends over a drink or some food, returning home in the early hours. And when I wanted an escape from indulging in city life, I would be off on holiday, exploring a new place or relaxing on a beach. Life was set. Two years later, I was single, homeless, living out of bags and desperately holding on to my job - I was depressed and at rock bottom.

The change in dynamics felt sudden and abrupt. After 8 years together, my partner decided that he no longer wanted to be in the relationship. So, whilst I was at work he changed the locks on our home, sending me a text as confirmation of the end of the relationship and ignoring all my calls for an explanation. Without warning, I had lost my partner, my home and most of my possessions. I was not prepared in the slightest. Not knowing what to do, I went back to my family home to try and gather my thoughts and make sense of the situation, as my brain scrambled to process what had happened.

The end of my relationship meant a quick end to the life I had been planning. Marriage – gone. Kids – gone. Exotic holidays together – gone. The home I had spent so much time and money on, lovingly decorating and organising – gone. We had spent so many years as a couple, building a future together, that our lives were deeply intertwined. Our extended families even took holidays together. There was nowhere I could go without someone asking about my significant other. There was nothing I could do, without thinking about him myself. From there, the destruction of my relationship had a knock-on effect to all the areas of my life. Family gatherings became anxious events. I tried to hide my situation but would be bombarded with questions about where 'he' was, how 'he' was and how 'his' family were. Friendships became strained on the surface level as I hid away, pretending to those around me that life was completely normal, unwilling to share my failure and disappointment with those close to me. Although work initially offered light relief through the routine and escapism, eventually, the façade began to crumble as I struggled to keep pace with the hard and fast work ethic I had previously enjoyed. I became immune to the daily work stresses; nothing could compare to the gigantic personal battle I was facing. I often found my mind wondering during meetings, internally screaming, "WHY ARE YOU TALKING TO ME ABOUT THIS! I LITERALLY DON'T CARE! MY LIFE IS FALLING APART!".

Every day my thoughts were loud and consistent: "How have I gotten to this point?"; "What could I have done to prevent the relationship breakdown?"; "Will we get back together"; "Will things ever be normal again?"; "How can I get back to the happy point in my life?". My mind would wonder around and around for hours. The questions, the thoughts and the confusion were non-stop. I tried to drown them out by focusing my mind on other things, like watching a movie, reading a book or listening to music. Despite this, my mind would creep back to the same thoughts I had been trying to escape.

Days turned into weeks and weeks into months – the time went by so painfully slowly and yet so quickly. Starting over was hard, each day consistently brought a new challenge which I went up against with varying levels of enthusiasm. Some days I would take small steps forward; focusing on the positive things in my life, no matter how small. Other days I would make huge strides forward, feeling happier, more self-assured and able to make plans for the future. However, there were many days I would fall backwards, feeling depressed, unmotivated and unsure of myself. Despite the challenges and backward steps, each day bought new hope for things to be better than the day before. Even though I did not know what the end picture would be, the small consistent steps forward eventually allowed me to positively re-evaluate where I was starting from in my life and what I wanted, without having to consider my previous relationship ties and obligations. I re-focused on the things that made me happy and were important to me, and I began to re-connect with people, goals and activities that were positive to my life.

As I started to get back on my feet and my life headed in a constructive direction, it was incredibly difficult looking back at the path I was on before my relationship broke down. Each element of that previous life felt on track at the time and I had the expectation that the path would lead me to the things that would verify a good and successful life – a family, a home and a good career. However, as I reconstructed every aspect of my new life, I began to see more clearly that my previous path was covered in cracks that were deep and destructive. Cracks that had been in place for years, which I had overlooked and desperately tried to patch up, skipping over huge crates in the road, in order to try and follow the path to my desired destination. I had been trying to make the best of a bad situation and as a result the road had crumbled beneath me.

The reality was that in my early 20s, I was living an unhappy life. I was in a serious relationship with a guy I had been dating for a few years, which I knew had no solid foundation or future, but I felt pressured to marry because it appeared the next step in our relationship. I had a job in a reputable, well known company, that looked great on my CV, but I had no real passion for my role and could not picture myself in any senior positions. My social life was buzzing, I would spend many nights getting drunk, eating unhealthy food, gaining weight and not being honest with my friends about the struggles I was facing in my life, my career, or my relationship. And when I was not indulging in city life, I would be off on an overpriced holiday I had spent all year saving for, only to be able to enjoy it for a short period of time, before heading back to the rat race.

[Survival Mode – The Aftershock]

Chapter One

Day One – What now?

Synopsis: Looking at what Day One is and the varying circumstances in which it can occur. As well as looking at what to do once you have realised you are at Day One.

"One of the hardest parts of life is deciding whether to walk away or try harder"

Have you ever walked a route you are not familiar with and along the journey had a thought to yourself that you are not heading in the right direction to get to your destination? Everyone reacts differently to this: some people will look around and make a swift diversion to a new route; some people will keep walking on, positive that they are heading in the right direction, even though it may not be the best or most desired route; And some will go back to a point which they are familiar with in order to re-evaluate and choose a better route.

This also happens in life. There are some periods where you are travelling a path and feel quite happy along that journey, but then doubt and a nagging feeling starts to kick in. You wonder if you're on the right track or if you're with the right companion. You wonder if the road will continue to be a difficult journey to walk or whether/when the path will become smoother. You then have a choice to make: quickly adjust and choose a different path; continue on the same path, with hope that the road will get easier on the way to your destination; or go back a couple steps and re-evaluate the land, before choosing a better route.

When I started hearing the nagging thoughts and doubtful feelings about the path I was on, I ignored it. My reaction was to push through, continuing to move forward because I felt that my direction would eventually lead to a great destination. At the time, I had been with my partner for a couple years and although we shared values about family and relationships, our approach to other aspects of life varied from a little different to radically different. From money and careers to religion, we found some common ground, but largely we had different approaches and opinions. However, that did not matter in the early days. We were just enjoying spending our time together, making memories and living life, so we agreed to disagree – happily travelling along the journey of life together, unsure of the final destination, nonetheless delighted to be walking it together. As time went on and our relationship naturally became more serious, we each started to define our destination and our expectations for the journey. The further along the path we travelled together, the more that topics of varying opinion and indifference became a battle ground for arguments. Despite this, we continuously tried to compromise, pushing forward and hoping that the road ahead would become easier to travel as time went on. After a few years, I knew my successful, picture-perfect destination would include a family, home and a great career – so in my mind, it made sense to head there with the person I had spent so many years with. In reality, the journey had become more difficult as time went on, with our differences of opinion growing wider and deeper cracks in the path we were walking - eventually we stood on opposite sides of the road, unable to fill the cracks and ultimately, headed in different directions.

There is a kind of limbo, where you realise that your relationship has some red flags or issues. Sometimes you choose to address them and work on a fix, other times you may ignore them, hoping they go away and do not grow into bigger issues. During this time you may consider ending the relationship, but your uncertainty keeps you hanging on, even if you have one foot out the door. The ending of a committed relationship is never easy, whether you are the one that ended the relationship, your partner chose to end it or it was a mutual decision. At some point you were devoted to each other, making memories and building a life together and the change can be devastating. The person you considered your best friend, who you felt you knew so well, is now unrecognisable to you. The memories that you once held so dear, are now bitter and painful to remember and the plans that you made for the future are no longer visible.

It would be so much easier for me to sit here and tell you that I recognised the end of my relationship and accepted it gracefully, with no regret. The truth is that I desperately tried to mend the cracks and continue on, even though I knew I was unhappy and on a path that I didn't want to be on, but at the time I didn't see a better option. We had spent years together, growing, learning and sharing memories – no-one knew me better. When my partner made the choice to end the relationship, carrying along the same path was no longer a viable option. I had no choice but to take a few steps back and re-evaluate the land. My circumstances had changed too much for me to quickly re-route and choose a new path. I didn't want to start over, I never chose to start over, but in the end I had no choice but to start over and it was the best thing I could have ever done.

[Day One – What is Day One?]

Day One begins when you have certainty in your decision to close the chapter and move on. Day One brings a new perspective. You recognise that the previous situation was not right for you and no longer wish to return to that period in your life. It does not mean that you are healed from the distress and destruction that chapter in your life has caused, but it does mean that you are ready to move on from it and you are willing to head in a positive direction, letting go of the people or things that hold you back from progressing. Day One will arrive at varying times for people: for some Day One may come even before they have acknowledged to their partner that the relationship is over; for some it will be the day they officially break up with their partner; And for others it may be days, weeks or even months after the initial break up when they recognise they no longer want that person or relationship.

"One bad chapter does not mean your story is over"

On the day that my partner dramatically ended our relationship, I did not accept it as the end. I considered that it was a serious breakdown of our relationship and communication. We needed time apart to re-evaluate our connection and improve it, but I did not consider it would be the very end of our relationship. In the weeks following I remained in an emotional and delusional state, thinking that we would work things out and as time passed, that he would realise how much better life was with me, rather than without me. I was wrong. Having lost my partner, my home and not being able to have access to most of my possessions, I struggled to adjust to the drastic change in my life and longed for the imperfect life I previously had. As the days and weeks went by, I lost hope in going back to my previous life and began to face my new reality, but a little dash of hope always remained until Day One.

In the weeks following the break up there had been a lot of anger and arguments between myself and my ex-partner. He had blocked my number, so I struggled to communicate with him and express my feelings in a way that I felt heard. In contrast when he called me I always answered, in order to open the line of communications and in hope that the situation could be salvaged. This meant I often received late night calls of him disrespectfully shouting and ranting at me about a subject he wanted to get off of his chest. Despite this being mentally and emotionally draining, I listened to his criticisms. But with each call my patience declined more and more, as he refused to have a two-way conversation and acknowledge his own short-comings.

The day I finally confirmed I no longer wanted to return to my previous life, was the day my ex spontaneously extended his rants towards my mother, a person who had sat quietly on the side-lines, offering me continuous support, but never interfering. His rant was completely uncalled for and thoroughly disrespectful. They say **"When people show you who they are - believe them." Maya Angelou.** Words said in anger may seem temporary, but it can also expose a person's true thoughts and feelings. From that point I knew I was done – my ex had become someone I did not like or recognise, and I felt completely assured in closing the chapter and walking away.

It does not matter how much time it takes someone to get to Day One – some will find the journey easier and quicker, some will find the journey harder and longer, everyone moves at different paces and faces different challenges in life. Just because one person can confidently close a chapter quicker than another person is not important and should not be compared. Your journey is specifically tailored to you, no one has had to walk in your shoes or on the same path, making the exact same decisions. What is important, is having the confidence to walk away and put an end to a situation not meant for you, not knowing what the future holds, but knowing that this is the end of the current chapter and that things will improve.

[What Now?]

After Day One comes the realisation that you are starting over. Quickly followed by a multitude of emotions: Fear, excitement, uncertainty and positivity, to name a few. Starting over can seem like a gigantic task – it's scary and intimidating. You are staring at an empty road ahead, with hundreds and thousands of miles to travel before you reach your destination. It can put even the most assured people off from taking the first step and starting their journey, but remember this: **"The journey of a thousand miles, starts with the first step"**. I'm not going to pretend it's simple – starting over is one of the hardest things you will ever have to face. You compare yourself to where you previously were, what you could have had and where you are in relation to your peers or people you aspire to be like – these questions and comparisons, only serve to bring doubt and slow progress. At every point in the road you are challenged, but challenges will be overcome and personal growth achieved along the way. It will be incredibly worth it.

That first step is important and by identifying Day One, you have already taken it. However, be careful not to rush the journey to try and make up for lost time or reach your destination quicker. Now is the time to completely reset and focus on YOU. The first few steps are key, you wouldn't run a marathon without planning and preparation, and this should be the same for your life. Make sure that you have everything you need to start the journey – mentally, physically and emotionally. Sometimes that will mean getting rid of people, things or habits that are not beneficial to your life and your progress. It may be ending your relationship with your ex, but it may also be putting an end to friends that are not truly supportive of you and lifestyle choices that hold you back from being a better version of yourself. Starting over is the best time to reset and re-evaluate your life, making sure you have the best circumstances to make positive changes and be successful.

You may not identify all the things that you need and do not need overnight, but continuously putting yourself at the centre of what you want and looking at the elements in your life that positively contribute or drain you, will help in the resetting of your circumstances and prepare you for the road ahead. These are the foundations and as long as you have looked after YOUR needs and wants, you will have enough fuel to take yourself wherever your heart desires to go. Without looking after YOUR needs first, you can find yourself on another road leading to nowhere or in a direction that is based on someone else's needs and desires.

"You can't pour from an empty cup. Take care of yourself first."

Planning and preparation are also important to make sure that you have learnt from the lessons of the past and are headed in a direction that you feel happy and passionate about. Part of this will involve looking back at the situation you were in before and reviewing where you went wrong. It can be easy sometimes to push the blame on someone else and quickly identify the mistakes they have made, not acknowledging that our actions could have contributed to the downfall of the relationship or circumstance. No one is perfect and it is important to truly reflect on the decisions and choices you made that could have been dealt with better and can be learnt from. Identifying areas of growth and improved understanding that you can work on for the future will enable you to experience personal growth. You will be able to react to these situations better in the future, or even avoid toxic situations that might come up again. If you do not identify these areas, you will find that you continue to be involved in similar situations and circumstances as before, therefore not allowing you to progress in the way you need to excel along your journey or reach your destination.

Although the situation may not feel like it yet, this is your chance to change your life around for the better. Moments of taking a few steps back and observing the land, ready to go again, are rare – so despite how you may feel, embrace the change and work to improve and transform the elements of your life that matter to you.

Chapter Two

Going through the motions

Synopsis: Dealing with feeling multiple emotions as you try to acknowledge the vast change in your life. How long this period lasts and listening to what's right for you and your wellbeing.

Going through the motions is what we do to survive – repeating the movements that our body naturally does, just to keep moving and avoid us from stopping. Because if we stop, we might not get started again. Wake up. Cup of tea. Shower. Get dressed. Go to work. Lunch. Continue work. Head home. Dinner. Shower. Scroll through phone. Bed. Sleep… barely. Wake up and do it all over again. It's lame, it's boring, there is no excitement. But that movement gets you through the day. Each small step is progress – it helps you to put focus on something else even for a short moment. In those short moments you don't think about the millions of things floating around in your head. Thoughts about your current situation, how you got to this point and how you are going to get back on your feet – instead, you are placing emphasis on getting the task at hand done. And with every day that passes those short moments grow longer, more frequent and contain more joy, until you're no longer going through the motions and you're taking the steps because you choose to, not because you have to.

The period of going through the motions is just as important as Day One – however, it is not just about 'Going through the motions'. During this period, as you try to adjust to your life transitioning, you will go through a variety of emotions, trying to make sense of the past and all the things that lead you to this point, whilst also starting to put a picture together of what you want for the future. This period should focus on you healing from the negative emotions and upset of past pain, which will in turn provide a strong foundation for you to restart and not be held back by previous hurt. The amount of time that you will spend in this period will completely depend on you – there is not a 'One fits all' on mental and emotional healing. Take as long as you need, go through the motions whilst you deal with your emotions – wallow if you need to. And when the time is right, you will be ready to move forward, stronger than ever.

"Sometimes it's okay if the only thing you did today was breathe"

As I came to terms with the demise of my relationship, I did very little each day. Monday to Friday, I managed to get up and go to work, acting like everything was normal, although I felt like I was dying inside. I remember a colleague standing at my desk talking to me about an issue we had on our department and I stared through them, as I recited in my head, "I literally don't care. Nothing matters to me right now. Please just hurry up and leave me alone". Conversations in groups were okay, because I could be a part of the discussion without having to be an active participant, however having one on one conversations were a different story. Finding the motivation to take interest in normal subjects was challenging me like never before, I just could not find the purpose. On evenings and weekends, I spent hour after hour sat on the sofa, that also doubled as my bed, running over all the things that had happened. Were there signs that the relationship would end? How could I have handled the situation better? How can we repair this and go back to normal? Whilst on these days my mind was manically active, my body was incredibly still – I managed to eat, occasionally shower and not much else. I did very little on these days and it was exactly what I needed.

As much as you may have to go through the motions, you still need time and space to think. Do not be afraid to take some time for yourself – without it you will likely make a mistake. You need the time to heal and evaluate the situation before coming to terms with the change. Not everyone has the same timeline, some need a couple days, others a couple months or years. Take as much time as you need – this should be dictated by you.

[Anger]

When your relationship is ending and you are going through the transition period, you can sometimes feel anger or hate - either towards your ex-partner or towards the situation. These emotions are natural and may feel considerably justified if you are dealing with a particularly frustrating person or situation. As much as these emotions may feel warranted, they can have a negative impact on you, even if they are aimed at someone else. Keeping these emotions at the forefront of your head and heart will mean that you have less tolerance and patience for all the people and things in your life, even if you do not mean to. The last thing you want to do is get into an altercation or disagreement that will make you feel more anger or even regret. If you come up against a situation where you feel anger, frustration and hatred building up, force yourself to walk away from it – take a breather. It's hard to walk away from a situation where you feel wronged and you want to express your emotions to the other person, but walking away is the best thing to do. Walking away allows you to positively take control and shows the other person that they do not have any power to keep you in that negative circumstance. Instead, release this energy in a productive way, in order to avoid your negative emotions building up internally and/or exploding externally. Focus your energy on positive activities where you can work these frustrations and energy out – this might be: a high energy activity like boxing, dancing or running; it be doing something creative like painting, gardening or cooking; it could be something as simple as sharing your thoughts with someone who will listen. Whatever it is, find what works for you and use it as an outlet for when it all gets too much.

In the days and weeks following my break up, there were several moments where I felt that I wanted to explode at my ex-partner and I felt that my actions would have been justified if I had showed him the full force of my anger, however in those moments I forced myself to think about the likely outcome of my actions – some of which, would have likely ended in a jail cell. Instead I chose to walk away from those situations in order to calm down. As I look back on these moments, I have no regret about the way I reacted and feel proud that none of the actions I took made the already difficult period worse.

"Hate - It has caused a lot of problems in this world, but it has not solved one yet." Maya Angelou

[Stress]

Stress is such a hard emotion to control. You try not to think about the situation that is causing you stress, yet you find your mind wondering back to the same topic at every opportunity. Even when you are trying to focus on something else or listen to what someone is saying, you end up missing the point of what's being talked about because in the back of your mind you are thinking about your stressful scenario. The constant cycle of trying to let go of the stress, only to be right back at the start is tiresome. Even through sleep there is little escape – you lie awake, desperately trying to dose off into the land of dreams, only to feel more awake than ever, with your mind doing circuits. When you finally manage to dose off, it's time to wake up and face the stress mind-battle all over again.

The best way I have found to deal with stressful situations is to identify whether I can do anything to change them. If I am not able to control the situation or the outcome, then I let it run its course and try to focus on the positive impact I can have, if any. Worrying about something that I have no control over is pointless because it will continue regardless of my efforts. If I do have some control of the situation or outcome, then I focus on what actions I can take to improve the position and turn things around. Focusing my energy on making the scenario better means that I have less time and energy to stress about the current circumstance and instead am placing emphasis on a positive outcome, which will come from my actions.

"The greatest weapon against stress is our ability to choose one thought over another"

[Depression]

On the toughest days I felt depression take over my mind. I felt I had completely lost control and I could not see the light at the end of the tunnel. I would spend hours looking out the window, unable to think of anything apart from how unhappy I was and how much I hated my circumstances. I felt numb; I felt stuck; I felt lost; and I felt like a failure in every sense of the word, and every part of my life. This was my rock bottom period – I couldn't see anything further than what was in front of me, and it was a complete mess.

Unfortunately, there is no magic formula for overcoming this – for me it took time to mentally adjust and focus on the positive things that I had in my life. The more I focused on the positive, the more I felt hope for the future and could start taking steps forward. Think about the things you have in your life that you are thankful for and what brings you positive joy. It does not have to be big, it can be as small as getting some fresh air and going for a walk. Spend time regularly doing the things that help to lift your mind into a positive place. It's a challenge, but the more moments you spend in periods of enjoyment and positivity, the less time you spend in periods of sadness and depression.

[Regret]
Regret is easy and useless. What's done is done – we do not have the ability to go back and change it, so why waste time regretting it. At the end of a relationship, you may regret the person you were with or the amount of time you stayed in that relationship. You may regret committing to that person or not following your gut feeling. Either way, we should not regret the choices we made and actions we took – each step and decision that was previously taken has led to the point

you are at now, and those past regrets are lessons, allowing you to identify what you do and do not want for the future. As long as you acknowledge those lessons of the past, they will guide you along the right path for your future. Without them you would not be able to witness the challenges you have overcome, the personal growth you have experienced and you would not be able to identify the changes you want in your life.

"I regret nothing"

[Fear]

When you are in the bubble of a couple, there is comfort in having someone to share life with. Being half of a whole, means that there is someone else who can take 50% of the responsibilities and help face the challenges of life. When you have to do it all by yourself, it can feel like a huge burden and can create fear. The fear of having to start over from the beginning. The fear of having to walk the journey by yourself. The fear of knowing there is such a long road ahead to get where you want to be. It is extremely overwhelming. Many times I have chosen to stay in bed and hide under the covers, unwilling to face my fears and it can be extremely tempting to stay there for an eternity. Some people have the ability to continuously face their fears, time and time again, pushing the limits, however others need some time to re-fuel, re-group and figure out an action plan before mustering up enough fight to push the limits. There is nothing wrong with taking some time for yourself before facing your fears – what is important is that your fears are not getting in the way of you reaching your desired destination. If your fears have become a blockade on your journey, then you need to face them and not let your fears hold you back. Only by facing your fears and challenges will you be able to feel the joy and excitement that comes from defeating them. With every obstacle you overcome you will feel more drive and motivation to overcome the next.

"The FEARS we don't face become our limits"

[Joy]

I love to laugh, it genuinely brings me so much joy to let out a laugh, whether it's at something big or small I usually find myself laughing at most things. At my lowest points I don't remember having the ability to laugh at all. Days and weeks went by where I felt I had completely lost the capability to find any form of enjoyment for life. I was depressed and felt that every topic was serious or irrelevant and to be honest, I was not much fun to be around.

It's hard to laugh in the early days, because you are consumed by everything that is going on, but things WILL get better. It might creep up on you slowly or it may come unexpected like a flash of lighting, but when that moment of laughter returns, live in it, embrace it, feel it within every fibre of your being. Put the distractions like your phone aside, forget about what you have to do later on, or the stresses of yesterday and breathe in that moment, because you deserve to enjoy that thing that genuinely makes you smile. That moment will feel glorious and you will be so glad for the return of that joyful feeling because it will remind you that there is so much hope and possibility for the future. Laughing is such a joyous emotion, so putting yourself in situations where you are more likely to laugh, such as being with friends or watching a comedy, will help to put you in a positive mind frame and bring more enjoyment to each day.

"The most wasted of all days is one without laughter"

[Closure]

Life would feel so much more pleasant if we were able to end every chapter with the closure we hope for and deserve. Wrapping everything up in a nice little bow and putting it to rest, ready to move on to the next phase of life. In the movies and on television, there always seems to be a story of closure – you find out how everything loops back and links together, you understand the impact of each scene on the ending and see how the characters move on with their lives. In reality, moving on without the genuine apology or closure that you deserve is usually the only option. You have to find your own closure to your situation, because if you do not move on, chasing the apology or closure will eat at you, and you will waste time and energy chasing something you may never get. Take control of the situation and choose to close the chapter yourself. Acknowledging the good, the bad and the ugly, then take the lessons from that period to move forward and build something better.

"And the truth is sometimes the only closure we can get from a relationship is time"

You may feel like your life will never get back to a positive place, but your circumstances will change for the better – stay strong. If you feel a heavy weight on you from: previous situations holding you back; not being where you want to be; or you may even be a few steps back from where you previously were – that's okay, your life will not be like this forever. It may not happen overnight, but you will get there - just keep moving forward. One step at a time.

Chapter Three

Self-Survival

Synopsis: Prioritising you: physically, mentally and emotionally. Making sure that you have everything you need to smile and get through this period. Looking at what you are thankful for, no matter how big or small.

Dealing with a large change in your life can mean your life feels like a jumble sale. Everything feels disorganised and erratic – your thoughts, your feelings, and you might even feel a mess physically. During the transition, whilst you are trying to come to terms with the change and you are unsure what your next steps are, it's easy to let the disfunction continue and overtake because it matches what you are feeling.

When I finally managed to get my possessions back from my ex-partner, I didn't know what to do with them. There was no space in my Mum's home to keep all the items I had built up over the years as part of my adult life after I had left home. My Mum had transformed the space where I had spent my childhood and teenage years, into a hub of relaxation, with lovely wooden furniture, books and trinkets, as well as some items I considered junk. I had enough space to keep a few of my clothes and key items, but not much else.

After several cab rides back and forth to get my items from my previous home, I closed the door on my Mum's flat which was now filled with binbags of my possessions taking up every space possible. I wanted to run and hide, to avoid the massive task that was in front of me, but despite my emotions, my Mum stood strong, making sure there was no delay in tackling the task ahead. She started cleaning and sorting, whilst I was in a daze, staring at the items I had gone without for months, thinking of all the memories each one held. We worked late into the night – nearly every item had to be washed or wiped down, due to being covered in mildew – possibly from where my ex-partner had bagged them up and left them in a damp cupboard or corner for months. The whole task was challenging, physically, mentally and emotionally, but as I sorted through the items I had spent my whole life collecting, I mentally sorted through my life and started to organise my future.

My best option was to pack away my belongings and put them into storage, so I did not want to pay to store any items that I no longer wanted or needed. I also knew the next time I would be unpacking them, it would hopefully be a positive occasion and I wouldn't want to sour the event with unhappy reminders. As I looked at each item, I thought about its purpose and its memories, then made the decision to keep or get rid of. Anything that unpleasantly reminded me of the life I had before, had to go.... Well, almost everything – I felt I had an obligation to keep pictures where I looked amazing! Even though my ex-partner tainted the picture with his presence. But those pictures were not for framing, they were placed in a box for the occasional reminder of a life before. I have never been a fan of destroying pictures. I always consider that in thirty or forty years' time, when I'm old and grey, looking back on the life I have lived, those memories may not be so hard and I may want a reminder of how things once were, even if some situations have not turned out as previously wanted.

Once my items were sorted and stored, my mind felt a lot clearer, and I felt more in control of my life. I still didn't have a plan for what the future would be, however the clarity gave me a better perspective of what it could be.

Taking the time to sort through the old in preparation for the new applies physically and mentally, whether it is clearing through old possessions or dissolving legal ties to your previous life, when you clear them out or organise them, you no longer have to think or worry about them. This may be at the bottom of your list of things to do, but once you have cleaned, cleared and sorted your life, you will feel a difference in your mind frame. The process also allows you to start from a fresh platform, free of reminders from your past life, that may ignite negative emotions, and it is another positive step forward on your new journey. If you are lacking in motivation to actually take the steps you need to sort things out, ask for help from someone who can support you in taking action. Having someone who cares about your wellbeing and can help in the process is invaluable when your drive is low. They may be able to offer an opinion on what to keep or how best to organise, but inevitably you have to be the one to make the decisions on what will happen to the items and links you have to your previous partner, because this is your life, your story.

[Prioritising You]

It's strange how the impact of doing something positive or productive can have an impact on our minds. I found that as I transitioned through the varying emotions of dealing with a breakup, days where I took the time to look after and focus on myself and my enjoyment, were the days that were easier. It began as little simple things – having a long, hot shower. The warmth of the water felt refreshing and cosy, the smell of the eucalyptus in the shower gel was calming and for a moment it grounded me – not thinking about the stress of the past or anxiety of an unknown future. Just here, just now, nothing else. As time went on I made bigger gestures to feel good about myself, such as going for a long walk or trying a new hair style. The walk cleared my head, allowing me to breathe in some fresh air and take in the landscape that I was previously too busy to acknowledge. The hairstyle helped me feel good about what I saw when I looked in the mirror and gave me confidence when I went out in public. Anything that allowed me to positively focus on myself or keep me grounded from all the noise in my head, I would make the time for. It may seem selfish to focus on yourself, but it is not. Take time for you and look after your own wellbeing – it's vital, it's survival. As much you may have people around you to support and hold you up, you have to be the person to make the decision to survive and keep going. This is just as true for your mental well-being, as well as your emotional and physical – they all go hand in hand and neither should be neglected by you. If you do not look after yourself, how will you find the energy and motivation to move forward?

Eventually as my outward smile matched my inner feelings, I felt more excitement for the future and eager to continue my self-love and empowerment in new ways, with friends and family for company. Any way that I could have a great time with the people close to me and also make a good memory – count me in. I said yes to nearly every new experience and did things I had never done before, some of which I will never willingly do again! I learnt that I am a terrible dancer, from attending a dance class and I learnt that having a professional massage feels strange to begin with, although incredibly relaxing at the end. But I laughed, I enjoyed, I had new experiences and I made new memories. All whilst effortlessly forgetting the tougher periods.

"No matter how you feel, get up, dress up and never give up"

Pampering yourself can be a good way to encourage a positive mind frame – as they say "looking good, feeling good". It could be as simple as having a shower with a beautiful smelling shower gel that helps boost your mood or it could be having a manicure or pedicure. Exercise is also a good way to increase endorphins and support strong mental health. This may be difficult when all you want to do is lay on the sofa, however if you can push through the desire to do nothing, even for 15 mins, you will feel the difference. Try to make these actions a habit – do them on a regular basis in order to form a routine of positive actions that trigger positive mentality. Your choice of action may be something completely different to what is listed below, but as long as it is having a positive impact on your self-esteem, it will support your growth and healing.

[Positive Pampering and Mind frame Ideas]

- **Hot relaxing bath or shower:** The water and warmth helps refresh your mind and body. Using products which you like, such as a bubble bath or a body scrub, will also help make this an enjoyable activity for you.
- **Manicure/Pedicure:** Sometimes feeling fresh can be as simple as looking at newly manicured nails or toes.
- **Massage:** I didn't realise how soothing these were until I was in my late 20s. Try it out and see if it works for you – you could book these regularly or once a year.

- **Washing and Styling your hair:** A new hairstyle may be a way to bring positive change and confidence about how you look and feel.

- **Going for a long walk:** It's amazing how fresh air can make you feel refreshed and grounded. I also find walking along a route I am less familiar with to be an interesting exploration of my neighbourhood and gives me something different to see.

- **Praying/Meditating:** Connecting with God, expressing your thoughts and feelings to him, asking for his help along your journey and letting go of your worries to find calm.

- **Exercise:** In any form that you enjoy – a marathon if you choose, or it could be a 10 minute workout that boosts your mood. Good for your fitness and mental health.

- **New or re-vamped clothes:** Something that makes you feel good and brings you confidence when you put it on. It does not have to be the latest designer item or have a high price tag – it is all about how it makes you feel.

[Ideas for New Things to try]
It can be big, it can be small, it can cost a fortunate or cost nothing at all. The key thing is to open your eyes and mind to new experiences and new possibilities:

- **Arts and Crafts:** Whether its 'Painting and Prosecco', knitting a scarf or building a town of Lego, challenging yourself to try a new skill can generate new interests or uncover hidden talent.
- **Dance class:** Dancing is not a strong point for me, but I enjoy how it makes me feel. Learning a dance routine was completely new to me and was interesting and fun.
- **Adrenaline activity:** Maybe getting your heart rate pumping is your thing. There are plenty of options to choose, from running a marathon, or rock climbing to ziplining, or even jumping out of a plane.
- **Spa weekend:** Going on a spa weekend with a group of friends and family is a great experience to share and one I really enjoy. We spent the weekend lounging around in cosy, dressing gowns, going from pool to sauna to steam room and then for a nap. And it was all the more special because we could enjoy it together.
- **Holiday:** There can be great excitement from the possibility of being able to explore a new place. Whether it's a staycation or a long haul vacation, changing your surroundings can be a good way to get some perspective on life and see new things.
- **Sell some unwanted items:** Every couple of years I enjoy going to a car boot and setting up a stall for things I don't

want anymore and I know could be valuable. For me, there is something about the hustle and bustle and the heated negotiations that I find incredibly stimulating. Plus, the search for anything of interest on other stalls.

- **Somewhere new to shop:** Spending the day shopping in a new location or environment is a great way to find new styles, designs or brands that you were unaware of. You could be exploring an out-of-town outlet store, a vintage store full of hidden treasures or a lane full of market-stalls.

"The things you take for granted someone else is praying for"

Be thankful every day for the good things in your life or the positive things that happened that day, even if they seem small. Did you manage to eat today? Did you manage to smile? Did you have a warm shower? Did you get the chance to enjoy some warm sunshine on your face? There are so many things that we are all hoping for, but do not forget to look around and appreciate the great things that you do have. Focusing on even the small things that you are blessed with gives new perspective and hope that even in the darkest of times there is light.

"Your terrible job is the dream
of the unemployed
Your house is the dream
of the homeless
Your smile is the dream
of the depressed
Your health is the dream
of the those who are ill
Don't let difficult times make you forget your blessings"

[Selfcare – Rebuilding and focusing on you]

Chapter Four

Re-evaluating

Synopsis: Evaluating what is important to you in the short term and what you need to get back on track. Or whether getting back on the same track is the right decision for you.

In the days, weeks and months following, many minutes will seem to be consumed by thoughts of your turmoil - what went wrong, why it went wrong and a million other questions. You will have moments where you manage to forget about what happened, but all too quickly your mind goes back to that situation. Going over the situation and understanding what went wrong can be a healing process, but it can also be consuming. Take your energy and evaluate what you do have in your life and what you are thankful for, then look at whether your life is how you want it to be.

"Don't sit in the dark and curse the dark. Light a match."

The rebuilding and evaluating phase requires a lot of internal questions to be asked and reflected on, but the core of this process is to look at whether you have everything you need in the short term to move towards what you want out of life. Look at the three elements in your life – these will be the framework for rebuilding your foundations and accelerating your journey in the short term:

1) Your passion: What do you enjoy? What is the thing you would be doing if time and money were not a factor?

2) Your grounding: What is the thing that forms part of your everyday foundation of being able to live your life? The thing that allows you to

fulfil your basic needs and gives you routine, but keeps you grounded from completely following your passion?

3) Your security: What makes you feel safe and secure in life? The thing or place that you can turn to when life feels messy.

When thinking about and choosing these key elements, it is important to focus on areas where you can make an impact as an individual, rather than relying on someone else to help you be completely fulfilled. For example, if your security comes from being with a set friends, then you are relying on those people to always be available when you need them, this removes the firmness from your foundation. Look at the portions of your life that you can control and take action in those areas.

Once you have identified these three areas of your life, think about positive changes you want to see in them. For example, if you enjoy your passion, think about how can you incorporate more of it into your life. You may want to consider if you are happy with your grounding and any positive changes you can make in this area to increase your happiness. You may also look at your security and consider if you want or need to feel safer in this area of your life and how that would be possible. All these thoughts and considerations will help you to evaluate what you have or what you want to achieve in the short term, which could be over a couple of months or a couple of years.

Use the answers to your internal questions to help you start to form some goals for yourself. Get a paper and pen, or pick up a device if you prefer, and start to formulate what you want from these areas of your life and build some plans around them. This may involve writing out what you want or it may be something visual like creating a mood board. Whatever method you choose, it will help cement what you want to change and act as a reference point to keep referring to when you need motivation of where you want to go. Evaluating these areas now, will provide motivation to improve your life. Whilst you may not have the big picture of where your life is headed, having plans and goals around your passion, your grounding and your security, will allow you to positively put focus and energy on the things you need and the things you can change. These are the parts of your life that will keep you engrossed and motivated on the tough days.

For me, as my life was transitioning, I chose the three elements that were important to me and I put my energy into these areas, whilst I positively planned for the future. I share these below to give you an idea of how you can approach your short term planning. Whilst these were perfect for me, your goals must be tailored specifically for you.

[Travel - My passion]

From a young age I have always enjoyed travelling to new places and gaining new experiences from seeing the world. Exploring a new place always made me feel so happy and full of excitement. In the days and weeks prior I would research, plan and organise with enthusiasm in anticipation of my new experience. Once I had arrived at my destination, I would spend hours upon hours wondering around, exploring where I was and learning about the culture and tasting the food. Then in the months following my travel I would reminisce by looking over the many pictures taken, or storytelling with the person or group I had travelled with, laughing and smiling at the great memories experienced. Due to the amount of enjoyment and happiness I got from travelling, I knew it would be a key part to building a life determined by me, but I also knew it would help re-find motivation and enjoyment in my life.

In my relationship, holidays required a lot of planning and aligning before going abroad, and I often felt I had to make many compromises about the places we could go and the types of places we would stay, because my partner had certain requirements for the types of places he would visit and stay at. Whilst I was open to exploring new places off the beaten track, my partner was insistent on always staying in a highly rated, all-inclusive hotel, which needed a mini fridge and room service. Don't get me wrong – I don't mind these types of luxuries and I definitely used his requirements as an excuse to spend more money than needed, once or twice. However, his requirements meant there were a lot of places which we could not explore together and in the end the compromise we had come to, felt more like settling on my part.

When I became single, I knew that by myself I would have the flexibility and opportunity to visit a variety of new places that my ex-partner would've objected to previously. However, I knew I didn't want to travel alone. I enjoy being around people I have a connection with and I feel that shared experiences are some of the best memories you can share with another person or group of people. The difficulty was that my closest friends were in serious relationships at the time, so weren't too interested in making plans for girl's trips. But I didn't let this stop me, I was determined to live my life to the fullest and I researched trips and retreats for solo travellers to join groups of other travellers. I found some great choices, however the high expense of these packages quickly made me reconsider the options available to me. It took some time to figure out the format that would best work for me, but my goal of travelling remained a priority. So I spoke to friends and extended family about their travel plans, seeing if there were any opportunities of me joining them, whilst also seeing if they were interested in the places I wanted to visit. As a result of my determination and speaking to people openly about my desire to travel I ended up enjoying group holidays in Dubai, New York and the

Grand Canaries, as well as Jamaica and The Dominican Republic with people I care about, making memories we will share for a lifetime.

Where do you want to go? What new experiences do you want to enjoy? You may know the answer to these questions fairly quickly, or you may need to take some more time to consider. Research and look at the various options available to you. There are so many different ways to visit or explore a country, you just need to find the way that is most enjoyable to you and brings you excitement. Through the process of researching and planning, you will start to think about what the ideal trip looks like and who it includes. You may even prefer to travel alone, potentially meeting new people along your journey or you may prefer to travel with a person or with a group from the beginning. Whatever you choose, it is entirely up to you.

When you have something you are truly passionate about, it helps to keep you motivated, but its not always easy and sometimes your plan may not work out exactly how you imagined. Be persistent about moving forward with your plans and goals – it could work out even better than you have imagined.

[Work - My grounding]
Like most people, I had to work to pay the bills and generally I didn't mind. I had a job in the city, which was always a good talking point,

and even though my role was demanding and fast paced I enjoyed the challenge. At some point before my breakup, I had become aware that I was likely the lowest paid in my department – it had never been an issue before because I had been offered a salary that was exactly in alliance with my expectations and was 30% more than I had earnt in my previous industry and role, but like they say "Comparison is the thief of joy" and as soon as I knew my colleagues were earning more than me, I felt less happy about where I was. So as my relationship was deteriorating, I was also in the process of finding a new job. I loved where I worked, but I was determined to increase my income and was ready for a new challenge. I had had some interviews for new roles and other companies, but the suburb locations made me uncertain about leaving city life behind so early in my career. A couple of months into my search, I was randomly contacted by a recruiter for an opportunity with a large tech company and I was already into Stage 3 of the excessive recruiting process when my marriage dramatically crumbled. I considered backing out of the process and trying to keep all the parts of my life that I could control stable, however I also had the feeling that it was now or never, and if I let the opportunity pass me by because of heartache, I would always regret it. So I put all my energy into practicing for the succession of five, 40 minute, back to back interviews – throwing on my biggest smile and trying to let my personality shine through, despite being at my lowest. I remember leaving the interview with a painful migraine and feeling exhausted, but I also felt empowered by the fact that I had performed well and completed the intense process. Additionally, I had spent half a day not thinking about the tragic circumstances of my personal life and that felt like a huge achievement in itself.

Work can be a great distraction when you have a personal struggle, as it allows you to think and focus on something else, but it can also be a struggle when you are dealing with difficult circumstances. It's not necessarily one or the other, it can be both to varying degrees. For me there were great days where I felt like I really smashed it, then there were other days where I felt like I was barely holding it together. As part of the re-evaluating process and looking at the things that bring you joy and excitement for the future, think about whether you are working in the industry or field you want to be in? Are you earning the money you deserve for your role? What can you do to change this? What can you do to get where you want to be? Evaluating what you want from your work can also benefit other areas of your life – for example, you may be interested in learning more negotiation skills in your role, which would benefit your knowledge and understanding in other areas of negotiation for personal purchases or future roles.

On difficult days, your grounding can sometimes feel like a chain, keeping you from truly living your best life in the way you choose, but the reality is that we all need balance. Without our grounding, would we enjoy our passions as much as we do? Grounding provides perspective and stability.

[Home - My security]

They say "Home is where the heart is", it is where you should feel safe and secure. The place where you can shut your door and truly be yourself. After being painfully evicted from the place I considered my home, sleeping on a sofa and living out of a suitcase for months on end became tedious. I wanted to change my circumstances and have a certain level of security in the next place I called home to ensure that I could never face the same uncertainty again, and to be in control of my own situation. At the time, I didn't feel that private renting would offer me the security I desired. I had always wanted to be a homeowner and had a keen interest in property, but after struggling to find an affordable property to buy with my ex-partner, I assumed it would be almost impossible to buy something on my own, and renting would be my only choice. I spent hours researching my options, looking at renting rooms, renting flats, the government backed 'help-to-buy' scheme and any other affordable options for a single person looking for security and independence in London. This was a long, difficult journey because there were so many elements of choice. Should I stay in the area I have known all my life or move away where it is cheaper? Should I rent a room in a sociable house or live alone? Furnished or unfurnished? I knew what it was that I wanted, but I had many questions about how I was going to be able to achieve this vision. As time went on and I kept my focus on researching and rebuilding this area of my life, the questions began to be answered and I gained more clarity about how I was going to achieve what I was searching for.

Wherever you find your sanctuary, do what you need to make sure it is a safe and secure place for you to let your hair down and feel comfortable to be you. If you are not happy where you currently are, think about what you need to make a positive change. Do you need to make the space feel more like yours? Do you need to move? You may not have everything you need right now to answer the question or build your vision, but keep working on it, eventually things will come together as you want and need.

The early steps of starting over and changing the direction of your life will be difficult – there is no denying that. There will be times when your mind drifts back to your situation before and you think: 'Am I doing the right thing?'; 'This would be so much better if we were doing this together' or 'I cannot wait to share this with someone significant in my life'. You might compare your new goals to your old goals and lifestyle or second guess your choices, this is normal. Keep re-evaluating along the journey, remembering what you want to bring forward from your last chapter, and what you want to leave behind.

Whilst also thinking about what your passion is, what your grounding is and where you find your security. Then be strong in your direction to obtain your goals. You will be amazed what you can achieve by yourself, and it will be all the more enjoyable to know that YOU made it happen.

Chapter Five

Re-focusing

Synopsis: Placing focus on the things that excite you and what you want in the long term. Looking at what you want to achieve and what the future looks like.

As you define your short term goals, you are creating the foundations of your new direction and providing the motivation to change your circumstances. These short term goals will provide an immediate focus for you and you may start to see new possibilities open up, things that you may have been closed off to before. New opportunities help us to see a new perspective in life and can also provide a positive change that we need, however it is important to know what you want in the long term. Knowing this is what helps form your journey and define your destination. Not every opportunity that comes your way will be right for you. Being able to define your long term vision allows you to understand which opportunities fit into your goals. This will help you advance along your journey, and recognise which opportunities will not help you on the way to where you are aiming to get to.

When you start over, although your circumstances and lifestyle may be vastly different to what you had in your previous chapter, it is unlikely that the things you value would have drastically changed. It is okay if your long term goals are similar to what you wanted previously, it is natural to desire and value the same things as before. Your long term vision may just be slightly altered to reflect your new starting point. What is important, is that your goal is based off a strong vision you have for your life, so it can inspire you on good and bad days, acting as a constant reminder and motivation of what you are trying to achieve.

[What is your destination?]

As you think about what you want in the long term, there are still many questions that you have to ask yourself, to help define your focus and destination for your life journey: What brings happiness into your life? What are you passionate about? What excites you? What do you want in the future? Where do you want to be in the future? How will you get there? There are a lot of questions which you may not initially know the answers to and that is okay. You may also feel overwhelmed by the many questions and aspects to think about and that is okay too. What is important is that you start to ask yourself these questions and answer them honestly, only then can you truly build the life you desire and deserve. The beauty in starting over is that you do not have to be confined to what is available to you – dream as big as you want and start on your journey to getting there.

"The moment you lose hope, you are just existing, you are not living."

Let's start with the big questions first: What makes me happy? What do I want from life? These questions are intimidating at first, but if you do not know your destination, then your route will lead you nowhere. Think about twenty years' time from now – what will you want your life to look like then? Think as big as you possibly can – do not be chained down by current commitments or life realities, such as work or money. Just think about what you would want to be doing if there were no limitations. Where will you be in the world? Who will you be with? How will you spend your time? What will a regular day look like for you in twenty years' time or will every day be different and spontaneous?

Twenty years might feel a very long time away, however having that vision of where you want to be by that time will help you to work backwards and plan the steps you need to take now to build that picture. As you think about that vision, think about what you need to achieve to get there. What are the goals or steps you need to take to reach that vision that you have for yourself. These must be things that you can impact - there is no point having a vision of winning the lottery because that is out of your control. Instead, the goal could be to earn extra income or grow your business to increase your disposable income and get you closer to that vision of having an abundance of money.

Write, draw or add images of your twenty year vision and goals here:

Next think about ten years from now and how you want your life to be. If you have a clear picture in your mind of where you want to get to in twenty years, then it will be easier to define the ten year dream, because it is half way towards where you want to get to. Continue to think big, do not be held back by the limitations of your mind or society - ask yourself the same questions as you did previously, but consider what you need to be doing at that point in your life in order to make sure your twenty year vision is on track. Also consider what goals you need to put in place now to support that journey.

Write, draw or add images of your ten year vision and goals here:

Now look at five years' time and where you want to be. Continue to ask yourself the same questions, looking at what you need to achieve to get there and the goals you need to put in place to align with your expectations for the longer term dreams you have set. Although five years is a lot closer to the present day, do not stunt your growth by being narrow minded - broaden your horizon, but be clear about what direction you are heading in to make sure you are on track towards your desired destination.

Write, draw or add images of your five year vision and goals here:

Three years from now – where do you see yourself? It's not that far away and yet it feels far enough away to not be daunting. A lot can happen in three years, so do not be afraid to have high expectations for where you want to be and what you want to be doing. As always, align your vision and goals to the chain of other longer term plans that you have for yourself and think about how you will get to the point you want.

Write, draw or add images of your three year vision and goals here:

Eighteen months from now, where do you want to be? This time period might be intimidating because it is so close. You may be tempted to be more realistic with your expectations and what you want to have achieved by the time you reach this point. Balance is important and having a realistic goal for what you can achieve in this time period would be sensible, but if you really think about it, things can change so quickly that what you want may be achievable in a year or even less. The important thing is that you know what you want and you can set the goals to achieve it in order to make steps towards reaching your destination.

Go back to the last chapter and look at your short term goals – make sure they align with your longer term goals. If they do not, take some more time to think about what you truly want now and what you want for the future, because without a firm direction, you are going nowhere.

Write, draw or add images of your eighteen month vision and goals here:

_____

_____

_____

_____

_____

_____

_____

_____

_____

_____

_____

_____

_____

_____

_____

_____

_____

_____

_____

_____

_____

If you want, you could continue to reduce the timeframes of the goals you have for your life down to a couple weeks. Some people choose to have a detailed plan of what they need to do every day, week and month to achieve their vision, whilst others may be more flexible, knowing what they want to achieve, by when, and continually working towards that direction. It completely depends on what works for you. The key thing is to stay connected to your dream in order to help you stay motivated and stay on track. By breaking down your vision of what you want for your life, you are planning your route to get there. You would not go on a journey without knowing your destination and planning your route, so why would you not do the same for your life?

Once you know the longer term vision of where you want to get to, you can then whittle down the questions into different areas of your life to really define and evaluate what makes you happy and what you want for the future. This may include looking at your love life, work life, relationships, spirituality, health, fitness, lifestyle choices, life experiences, the list is endless. As you put in place the plans and details to the vision you have for your life, it will give you different elements to focus on and it will help you in taking steps in moving forward to a future that you have defined.

When you are rebuilding your new life, it is natural to compare your new life to the plans, dreams and expectations you had of your life with your previous partner – even if it ended badly, there would have been good times when you would have been making plans and building a life together. These comparisons can make the process of rebuilding difficult and depressing, but embrace this change. It gives you the opportunity to do things your way, without negotiation – it's all about you and you deserve to live your best life.

Remember: **"The future doesn't care if you believe in it or not, it will arrive regardless."** So take the time and shine a light on the things you are positively passionate about and make plans for the future that will aid you in rebuilding a life that you want. Follow your intuition - your gut, if it doesn't feel right, it probably isn't. When you are starting over, you are starting a fresh page, a new chapter. Previous ties and obligations go out the window. All the things you previously had to consider should be forgotten – it's completely about you and what you want limitlessly, not what you want based on what you currently have available to you.

Chapter Six

Re-connecting

Synopsis: Looking at community and support systems and why they are important. Why it's good to communicate and the different roles that the people within your community play in your life.

"No one gets where they are on their own, each and every one of us has a community of people lifting us up"
Michelle Obama

When you are going through your journey of adjusting to life changes and discovering what you want for yourself, you can feel very alone and secluded from the people around you. You may feel that they do not know what you are going through or how you are feeling. The truth is, no-one knows what it's like to walk in your shoes and be you, but many can empathise with your circumstance and there are many people who may have been in a similar situation previously. On the road of changing your life and going after what you want, you are the centre and everything revolves around what you need and what you need to do to get to your destination, but you do not have to walk that journey alone – in fact, you should not walk that journey alone. Having company or a community of people who you can connect with, who support your vision and goals will make the journey that much easier and so much more enjoyable. These are the people who: will listen to you when you need to share your feelings or vent; offer advice when you need to hear words of guidance; belly laugh and celebrate with you in the good times; and/or hold you up when you cannot do it for yourself.

When people journey to the peak of mount Everest, it's considered ludicrous and dangerous to do it alone, and it is the same approach to life. Community provides uncountable benefits to enable you to learn and grow as a person, but also feel a place of belonging from people who value you, and value the same things as you. There will be periods when you will have to walk your journey alone and rely on only yourself to keep moving forward, but your community will be on the side-lines cheering you on as you take each step forward.

"In life: Good people bring happiness; Bad people bring experience; The worst people bring a lesson and the best people bring memories."

[Who is your community?]

The one thing that all your community will have in common, even if they never meet, is that they connect to you in someone way and they bring value to your life. The people that will make up your community will come in numerous forms: they may be a person who you know professionally, like a friend from work; or someone who you know socially, like a group that you play sports with or your best friend from childhood. They could be people that have been in your life for a long time, such as a family member or someone who is only in your life for a short period, like a stranger you meet randomly on a train and get talking to, then never see again. They could be someone that you know in-person, and meet up to hang out with, or they could be someone that you know virtually and only connect with via social media. Your community will be vast and mixed - it is rare that one person or group will provide all the support or guidance you need – different people and groups will provide a variety of diverse thoughts, perspectives and experiences, and like a patchwork quilt, those interactions will come together to provide a tailored comfort and support blanket that you need to lift you up and keep you going.

Over time, people will come in and out of your community as they will provide varying value, at different periods of your life. They can be segmented into three different types of people: 1) People who will have an unreplaceable impact on your transformation as a person, offering continuous love and support, without asking for much or anything in return, and often in your life for long periods of time; 2) People who offer love and support for a medium period in your life. Helping you fulfil your vision, but also requiring similar from you in their life; and 3) People who are only in your life for a season. They are not necessarily supportive of you and your destination – the relationship is transactional, where you are able to offer each other something for a required period. Each connection provides some value to your life – it will not always be happiness and memories, there will be some interactions that result in experience and lessons, but there is still benefit to you from that exchange.

"Alone we can do so little; together we can do so much"
Helen Keller

In my family, I was blessed to grow up with examples of strong, independent, family orientated women, as well as confident, entrepreneurial, motivated men. These are the people I watched navigate the blessings and challenges of life; the people I learnt from as they planned and chased their dreams; whilst staying connected to their family values. These were the people that had an unreplaceable impact on my life. One of the biggest things I learnt from my family is that things do not always work out in the timeline you want or expect, and it's almost always never easy, but if you stay focused on your goals, keep taking positive action towards them and surround yourself with people that help hold you up when times are difficult then you will get there.

[Reach out and connect]

Getting divorced in your 20s is such a weird experience – in the time when many of my friends were starting to settle down and get serious with their partners, I was entering a new phase of my life that none of my friendship group had experience of. I searched for blogs and influencers who aligned to my experience and found extraordinarily little that related to the break up with a long term partner in your 20s to 30s. Instead, what I mainly found was content written by middle aged women, who I could not relate to in the same way.

One thing I did find via a comedian on social media, was an Instagram account run by an anonymous influencer called Lala, who talked about dating and relationships. I started following Lala's page and found interesting opinions and advice from the posts, but what really made the account an incredible forum was that every Friday night, Lala would host an Instagram live with a black screen to keep her anonymity. During the live chat, Lala would discuss her own dating stories experiences, whilst also discussing the stories and dilemmas of the followers who had contacted her. Lala had a London accent which was relatable to me because I grew up in London and have a fondness for Londoners, but her experiences were also very relatable and her advice was always supportive and straight to the point. The regular live chat created a community of women who gave encouraging comments and thoughts to uplift each other; and offer support through difficult stages in their lives. Every Friday night I looked forward to tuning into the Instagram live and hearing the anecdotes. It's strange to think that although I never shared my story, this community of anonymous women, and some men, helped me through a low point in my life, but each week it reminded me that there are many people going through difficulties and I was not alone in feeling heart broken. Community, in whatever form you find it, is especially important in making sure you have the positive support you need to enable growth and get back on track.

If you feel like you do not have the community and support that you need, take action and go in search for like-minded people. This could involve joining a club, doing something you enjoy with other people who enjoy it. It could be joining an online community to talk about topics with like-minded people. It could be joining a church group or starting a course. Or it could be speaking to a therapist to help you work through your thoughts and feelings, whilst getting professional support. Even if you feel a little nervous about meeting new people there are lots of different options available, you just need to explore the possibilities and do what feels right to you. Who knows, you might even end up meeting a new love interest! Now be realistic - you are unlikely to find the man of your dreams sitting at a knitting club every Wednesday evening, with a bunch of ladies in their 80s, talking about the inflation of biscuits over the last five decades. But vice versa, you should not be hanging out at the local building merchants if you cannot tell a Philips screw from a nail and have zero interest in DIY. The important thing is that you spend your time doing the things that you genuinely enjoy, and as a result you will naturally meet people with similar interests, whether that's new friends or new love interests.

[New Relationships]

Entering a new romantic relationship after one has ended, is different for everyone. Some may feel they're in a position to re-enter the dating scene soon after their last relationship has ended, for others it will take longer. Everyone's situation is different and there is no, one size fits all. Take as much time as you need or do not need. You are fully in control of this aspect of your life and should do what feels right for you.

When I re-entered the dating scene, it was a completely new experience for me - I spent my late teens and early 20s in a relationship, so I didn't really understand what it was like to be single and date. Online dating had become such a big phenomenon that many people of a similar age to me spoke about and were exploring, but I had no experience with it at all. It took some time, but eventually I felt in a place where I was ready to move forward and open to meeting someone new. From the beginning, I was clear on the type of people I wanted to meet and what I wanted to achieve from the situation and because of that, I could easily discount the type of platforms I would use to connect with them, and the type of person I would meet in reality. Don't get me wrong – it wasn't always straight forward, there were many trials and errors in searching for the right platform that reflected my values and worked for me. There were times when I wasted time speaking to people I had no interest in, out of sheer boredom; or thought I had met someone great, only to find out we didn't have a romantic connection. Each time I reminded myself of the type of person that I wanted to meet, who shared my values and interests – some people may say you need to compromise, and I feel that may be true in some respects, but it's important not to settle for something or someone that doesn't align to your vision for your life. If the situation isn't right, don't be afraid to be independent until you find someone you truly connect with.

"A woman who knows what she brings to the table is not afraid to eat alone."

[Share your struggle]

For six months, only my closest family knew the heartache I was dealing with. Whilst I thought that I was hiding my turmoil from friends and family and acting like life was normal. When I finally had the courage and certainty to reveal what I had been going through, many of them shared that they could see I was not myself, but they were unsure how to approach the situation. The truth was that they could see the agony in me, but were giving me the time and space to be honest about what was going on in my life. Once I stopped hiding the secret of my situation, I felt like a weight had been lifted from my shoulders, I no longer worried about keeping up appearances and could express how I genuinely was feeling. I shared my story, with reactions of shock and disbelief from my friends and family, but at the core was an abundance of love and support that was a huge help in closing the chapter and moving forward on my journey.

"There is no greater agony than bearing an untold story inside you" Maya Angelou

Part of community is the ability to communicate and learn from each other. Do not be afraid to speak about your story with those you trust and will support you – It can be a good way of healing and they can offer you help and advice that you may not have been aware of. However, if they do not know your stories and your struggles, they cannot offer you anything. So don't do what I did and hide away from the people who genuinely care for you, talk to them about the challenges you're facing, and you might be surprised at how, by being honest and open about your situation, you will feel different, but also receive invaluable support.

Chapter Seven

One step at a time

Synopsis: Why taking action is key to moving forward. Getting started, being consistent, overcoming humps in the road and celebrating your wins.

Knowing how you want to change your life or what you want to achieve in your life can be a powerful motivator. Those dreams and ambitions can give great hope on difficult days and the plans you make can outline the journey of how you will get to where you want to be. However, nothing can be achieved without taking action. Implementing the plan you have to achieve your goals is how you will fulfil the vision you have for your life – taking one step at a time, you will move closer and closer to your dream with every action taken.

One thing that was key to me in my vision for the change in my life was finding my security, for me this came in the form of a home of my own. I knew what my end goal would look like, however I didn't have clarity on how I would achieve it. I spent weeks researching the different, affordable options of purchasing a property that were available to me, yet I was no clearer in knowing which one I would use. Eventually, I became tired of researching and started taking action: I spoke to Mortgage Brokers who assessed my financial situation; I called Estate Agents, booking viewings for affordable properties; and I viewed dozens of potential homes, putting offers on every single one. With each house I would get excited at the possibility of a new home and how I would make it mine: I would picture the walls painted in the colour I liked, with furniture that would fill the room and make a cosy space. However, with every offer came a rejection and the disappointment that I had to look for something else.

This process continued for months – I would spend evenings and weekends searching for and visiting any property that I could afford and could get a viewing to see, but every time I was faced with the disappointment of elimination. After some time, with a pile of rejections and house prices rapidly rising, I became discouraged by the process and questioned whether I would ever achieve my goal of finding a home, however despite how hard it was, I knew that staying in the same circumstances would be more depressing and disheartening. So I remained consistent in taking action and finally I had an offer accepted on a home that had everything I had been looking for.

I would love to say that after my offer was accepted, everything was smooth sailing, but it was not. I continued to face challenges in the process, from not having a good enough credit record, to not having a big enough deposit. It was tough and some days I didn't know how or if I would overcome the barriers that appeared to be blocking me - at each point I reminded myself of what the end vision was and focused on the step I was trying to overcome at that time. It was challenging, but when I finally completed the buying process, it felt as though every hurdle had been worth the challenge. I had achieved my goal of owning a property, provided the safety and security that I craved, whilst reminding me how far I had travelled since my relationship breakdown. I knew I still had so much further to go before my home was comfortable and liveable, however achieving that goal put a smile on my face for months and kept me motivated in achieving other goals on my list.

"You miss 100% of the shots you don't take"

[Take the first step]

It all begins with the first step. We have been taking first steps for a lifetime, throughout different chapters of our lives. From our first step as babies, to our first steps into school, our first steps into a job and our first steps into being in a serious relationship. There are many first steps we have taken during our lives that we have forgotten about – At the time, we were filled with excitement and nerves, or maybe feeling a little anxious, as we were faced with a large change or a new chapter. Years down the line, we look back and see how far we have come since those first steps that felt like a huge, character defining statement at the time, where you overcame the uncertainty of change and grew as a person.

Deciding what you want for your life and making the changes required feels just as daunting in your adult years as dealing with change when you are a lot younger. The only difference is that you can look back at the first steps you took as a child and realise how much smaller those steps seem with age and experience on your side. Take a moment and think about how you would support your younger self, dealing with the nerves and anxiety of a change that you know worked out for the better in the end. Now think about what the future 'you' would say to the you right now. Will you look back at this time and wish you had not hesitated on making the decision, and taking action to improve your life?

Be careful not to hold yourself back - sometimes we do this without realising we are limiting our capabilities, because we are risk adverse or afraid. I have seen so many people give up on their goals before they have even taken the first step. Blocked by their own concerns and doubts. Take the first step, then take the next step and keep pushing forward. If it's not meant to be, learn that through experience and learn through the lessons that come from it. The worst thing you can do is have a plan or vision and not take any steps to fulfil it.

"Your future is created by what you do today, not tomorrow"

It can feel somewhat comforting to make the commitment to start but off-putting to take the first step. Internally, you might tell yourself

"I'll do it tomorrow" or "I'll start a fresh from Monday", or maybe you are waiting for everything to feel right. The truth is the delay is just an excuse to avoid taking action and getting the task done. There may be many reasons why you are delaying and you may have a genuine need to give yourself a break from starting, but the majority of the time you will be causing yourself unnecessary delay to starting something that will benefit you in the long run, so stop making excuses, remove distractions and get started.

[Tell Someone]

When you have a goal that you are working towards, you may feel excited about what you want to do and want share it with others. Sharing your goals and ambitions with a person or people who you know, can be beneficial to helping you along your journey. They may be people in your community that you want to talk to about what you are aiming for, who will be supportive and encouraging of what you are trying to achieve, especially on tougher days. Or you may choose to select a mentor or mentors - people who have been on a similar journey as you or come through similar challenges. Whoever you choose to tell about your dreams and your goals for achieving your vision, the key thing is that by sharing what you are aiming for, you are no longer only committed to your internal promises to yourself. By saying them out loud you have made an external commitment with someone to witness and acknowledge, whilst also making yourself accountable. In addition, you now have someone in your life who may ask you about your progress and serve as another reminder that you are working towards your goals.

[Be consistent and overcome hurdles]
They say the first step is the hardest and it is definitely challenging, however being consistent is just as difficult. Taking action day after day, sometimes with no improvements, no results and no positive change, can be demotivating, depressing and boring. During this period, it is most likely that people give up on their dreams – they have taken some action, but they can no longer see the end destination in sight and have lost motivation to carry on. They might fall back into old habits and routines that offer comfort and familiarity, avoiding the difficult steps of making a change. The reality is that change is not easy and nothing worth having will happen overnight – it takes hard work and dedication to achieve the things you want to achieve, and you will face many hurdles and some dead-end roads.

"Just because something is difficult it doesn't mean you shouldn't try, it just means you should try harder"

At times you may be doubtful of being able to achieve your goals. You may be concerned that your journey will end in failure. Keep reminding yourself of why you want the change and what that end vision will look like – you only fail when you give up on that end vision. It is okay if you set a goal and do not reach it in the timeframe that you want or expect – what is important, is that you took some steps forward towards hitting that goal. When you truly want something you should never give up on it – it may not come in the exact form or timeframe that you want or planned for, but if you are committed and remain consistent in taking action to reach your goal, you will make progress and eventually achieve that goal.

The plan you made for your vision of where you want to get to in life is broken down into different stages and helps provide goals and direction for achieving your dreams. This helps form a good basis for a plan, but you cannot prepare for every circumstance or eventuality. There will be times when you do not know what is ahead in your journey or you may not feel you have everything you need to take the next step, but do not stop – keep taking action and focusing on the current steps you need to take to move forward. You may have to work out what the next step is whilst you are along the road – just keep faith that the challenge will be overcome and you will figure it out.

[Celebrate]

Achieving one of your goals or hitting a milestone on the path of reaching your goals, is a key point in any journey. It can remind us how far we have come and show us how far we must go to reach our final destination. Once you tick off one goal, you may be tempted to quickly move on to the next in order to try and reach your destination quicker. We are sometimes so consumed with where we are trying to get to, that we fail to truly acknowledge what we have accomplished and fail to embrace the present achievement. Celebrating what you have now, allows you to enjoy what you currently have and feel good about the hard work that helped you achieve it, whilst also boosting your motivation for the next goal. Your celebration could be big or small – you may want to throw a big party for everyone you know or you may want to enjoy your favourite meal with your closest friends. Whatever you do, make sure it is something you enjoy and will remember with delight in years to come.

"Do not judge me by my successes, judge me by how many times I fell down and got back up again."
Nelson Mandela

[Glimpsing back, whilst moving forward]

Chapter Eight

Life Lessons

Synopsis: Looking at the positive elements from the situation and how there can be lessons in some of the most difficult circumstances. Learning to look back and acknowledge that periods of change and challenge is where you grow the most.

"Change is hard at first, messy in the middle and wonderful in the end."

Depending on what stage you are at in your journey, you may or may not be able to acknowledge lessons from the previous chapter in your life. In the beginning stages, when you are initially starting over, you may still crave the life you lived in your past relationship, wishing everything would return to how it was before. Or maybe you feel that the change was right, but the adjustment to your new circumstances is hard. The first stage will always be the hardest period – this is where your emotions are still fresh from that relationship and it takes time to overcome those feelings.

As you move on from the break up, you will begin to recognize elements from your previous relationship that you were not happy with and that needed to change, but feel overwhelmed by all the different emotions and thoughts you have of the past, whilst still trying to adjust to what you want for your future. This middle stage is the longest – dealing with feelings of the past, as well as trying to make positive plans and take positive action for your future. You will have days where you feel low and feel like you are back at the start of your journey, and you will have days when you feel as though you have made great progress and you are at the end of the turbulent road.

As that transition period ends and you have moved on from the heartbreak and hurt of the past, you will look back and see everything that was wrong with that relationship and what led to its demise, while also being grateful that it came to an end and your life has changed for the better. This is the beautiful period, when you can see how far you have come and the personal growth you have achieved through the challenges of change.

Remember this quote as you deal with various obstacles in your life: **"Sometimes the hardest thing and the right thing are the same"**. There will always be difficult periods to overcome, but you will get through it and you will be grateful that you went through it, because it will lead you on the right path, despite the challenges. Additionally, without the hard periods you would not be able to recognise the great periods - comparison is what makes the great times so much more enjoyable and worthwhile.

[Reviewing]

It's okay if you look back and there are things that you wish you had addressed earlier or things that you would have changed. At the time you were living in that phase of your life, you did not know what you know now – you may have had hope for a better ending or you may have been naïve to the reality of the situation. You may have also made poor choices, which you knew at the time. We have all been there at some point and we all have things from the past that we would change given a second chance. It can be hard to face up to the mistakes we have made – it forces you to look at yourself honestly and acknowledge where you have fallen short. The important thing is that we learn from what has gone before, because the lessons we learn enable us to grow into better people and make better decisions in our lives, which inevitably, creates a better outcome for ourselves in the future. These lessons will also stick with you throughout your life as you have to make various decisions and potentially face similar situations again, so take the time to truly understand and absorb what you have learnt from this chapter.

"Growth was never meant to be comfortable"

Each person will take a different learning from the same situation, so it is key to know what you have learnt and how you will apply the teachings to your life going forward. For me, as I went through the journey of rebuilding my life, there were four key things I identified about myself and the way I want to live my life going forward. These help me to remember what is important when I feel I am getting off track:

[Embrace and nurture positive relationships in your life]
When you are in a committed relationship, it is easy to get drawn into the world of 'each other'. You spend more and more time together, and you may find that you do not have as much time as you once did for other relationships in your life. Whether you are in a committed relationship or not, it is important to embrace and nurture all the positive relationships in your life as best as you can, especially the people who are integral to your life. These are the people and connections that you will have a laugh with and encourage you in tough times, so be careful not to neglect them in good times. The connection you share will not grow and develop if the relationship is not nourished and nurtured.

The lessons learnt during this phase of your life may directly relate to romantic relationships, however not all the lessons will relate to that interaction. There may be learnings about how you deal with relationships in general, from family to close friends or even acquaintances. There may be lessons about how you deal with difficult situations or how you deal with change. Whatever the lesson is, take the time to understand where things were wrong or could have been improved, and think about how you would develop a better outcome if you were to face a similar situation in the future.

[Live for the moment, but plan for the future]

We have no idea what is around the corner – it could be something great or it could be a difficult challenge. There's no point in worrying about what may or may not happen, but we should be prepared for it. We have to live for the moment that we are in, whether it is a good phase or a phase that could do with some improvements, and planning for the future is smart. We can sometimes be so consumed by the period which we are in, that we forget to plan for what may be ahead. You are still on the road to your destination, so without planning and preparation, you will not achieve your goals. Find the things that bring positive joy to your life and embrace them, put your phone down and live in that moment of happiness and feel the feeling of contentment wash over you – then look at your goals and make sure you are taking action towards them.

[The other side of your challenge is either a victory or a lesson, both are good]

I truly believe that there is always a lesson in everything we do, especially when things don't go the way you planned or wanted. It may be hard to see or understand at times, but if you face your challenges with the certainty of knowing that if it doesn't work out, you still would've gained knowledge from the situation, you'll find that your confidence levels massively increase. Instead of being worried and stressed about what could go wrong, you are motivated by what you are going to gain from the experience. Not everything will work out how you want – it could turn out terribly or sometimes it will work out better than you could have even imagined, but you don't know until you have been through the trials and tribulation to come out the other side.

In a stage of my life when I was at my lowest, I pushed through all the hurt, pain and depression to complete one of the most intense interview processes I have ever known and secure a role with one of the fastest growing, and well-known companies of my generation. In the end, the victory was not the job or working for a prestigious company – the victory was pushing forward during the dark period to find and create an opportunity in spite of my situation, and take steps forward on the journey of my new life. That situation taught me that I can achieve anything if I put my mind to it and keep taking positive action, no matter how I may feel. Not everyone will have the same lessons from life – all our experiences are fairly unique, but we can still learn from each other's lessons and experiences to help teach and motivate ourselves.

"What we place our hope in influences our ability to endure difficult times. If we cling to something that is taken from us, our lives will crumble"

[Believe in yourself]

When you look at what you want for yourself, do not let doubt or new obstacles restrict you from achieving what you desire. Have faith that you can achieve what you have set out to do - believe it with every step you take and every challenge you come up against. You are your own biggest supporter, so if you do not believe it can be done, no one else will expect it can be done either. If you find it difficult to genuinely believe that you can achieve what you have set out to do – think about the last time you overcame a big challenge and keep reminding yourself of that success to keep you motivated. If you did it once, you can do it again. Eventually you would have achieved the thing that you set out to do and will be amazed at how far you have come on your journey.

"She believed she could, so she did!"

Along your journey you will also experience additional positive outcomes that you may never have expected, such as new skills and/or confidence you have gained along the way. In my relationship, I relied on my partner to deal with certain aspects of our lives, which led me to completely be dependent on him to make the decisions in those areas. At the time it made sense that we shared our lives in that way, as it meant each of us did not have to deal with the things that we were less familiar with, or had little interest in. Being single and independent forced me to gain new skills and knowledge in a variety of areas that I never expected I would need but have been invaluable to my growth. I moved to a new town where I didn't know anyone and had to create a home and community. I have had to negotiate and hire builders to renovate my home, communicating about the style and design, the work needed, timeline and payment, despite not having any experience in this region previously. I have travelled solo, 24 hours one way to Asia, navigating the transport system in a country where I didn't know the language to find my way around. These may seem like small achievements to some, but they were massive triumphs and huge learning experiences for me. I would take on these challenges again, with little hesitation, however there was a time when these tasks felt like a huge obstacle to take on by myself. Apply yourself to your new life and believe in yourself to do the things that you want to do, and see what skills, experiences and confidence you gain.

"Great testimonies come from great tests"

The most challenging chapter of my life so far, has become my greatest success story of overcoming adversity, and is my source of inspiration on difficult days. Everyone has periods in their life where they are uncertain about what the future holds and can feel unsure that things will improve – on these days: remind yourself of the great tests and challenges you have previously overcome; remember the lessons you have learnt and how you have grown as an individual; and let these be a motivation for you to keep moving forward.

Chapter Nine

Self-Love

Synopsis: Why it is important to continuously look after and prioritise yourself and your needs first. As well as looking at the impact you can have on your relationships by being your best self.

[Keeping YOU in the focus]

In times of distress it's natural to focus on you, because you are focused on survival: You think about what you need to heal from any trauma in your previous situation; You think about what you want for yourself in the new phase of your life; And you think about how you are going to get back on track. When you are unhappy, going through the motions and adjusting to the closure of a chapter, there is not much you can offer anyone in your life. You become the focus, and because of that, all your needs and wants are tailored specifically for you, with the aim of getting you to a point in your life where you feel happy and positive.

As you start to feel happier in yourself and more confident about where you are in your life, continue to make time to look after your needs and wants. Finding the time could be an hour a day, one day a week or five days out of the week. You could spend that dedicated time: listening to your favourite music uninterrupted; having a manicure/pedicure at your favourite salon; or working on your business idea that you are excited about – it completely depends on what you feel is right for you. If you are spending days and days dedicating time and energy to something that you are not passionate about, and you feel it's taking time away from what you want to do, then pause and re-evaluate. You can say no to something that does not fit in with the dreams and desires you have. As long as you feel fulfilled and you have time that is dedicated to you, you will feel happier and internally satisfied because you know you have devoted some time to yourself and your needs.

Finding time for yourself also benefits the various relationships you have in your life. The time and energy that you dedicate to healing and looking after yourself allows you to be a better person, and in turn you are able to contribute more to the relationships around you. For example, when you are feeling internally happier and more confident, you are more likely to notice when someone around you is having a difficult time. Therefore, you are able to address the situation and potentially help them through it. Whereas, when you feel unhappy and unsatisfied, you may be so consumed with your own circumstances, that you are less likely and less willing to spot if someone close to you is having a tough time, potentially causing a strain on your relationship, without realising why.

Focusing on you does not mean disregarding or not recognising others feelings and struggles. You can focus on your needs, whilst also being a supportive and loving person in other people's lives. It just means you should not consume yourself with other people's needs, without acknowledging what you also need in your life. There may be times when you do need to prioritise someone else in your life, but you will be better placed to support them if you are also looking after yourself. As with all things in life, having a healthy relationship with yourself and other people requires balance – Just do not forget to include YOU in the equation.

[Mental, Emotional and Physical Health and Well Being]

They say 'health is wealth' and health is a key part of our lives. Being a healthy person requires looking after your mental, emotional and physical health – All three are important and help you to operate at the top of your game. It is very normal when we're not feeling physically well, to book a doctor's appointment and ask the doctor to check what the problem may be. We sit in the Dr's office listing all the symptoms and potential causes, hoping they will find the root of the problem and provide a cure. It is however, less common for us to seek help when we are not feeling mentally or emotionally well. We ignore the symptoms, conceal the potential causes and disregard possible cures. All three types of health are linked and need to be looked after equally – Neglecting your physical health, can have a knock on impact to your mental health, which will have an impact on your emotional health. For example, gaining weight can cause people to feel less confident about themselves, which can cause them to feel shy about going out and socialising. Whereas exercising regularly and eating balanced, healthy meals, can help us to feel more confident, as well as mentally fit. It also works the other way round – If you are feeling upset or down, you are less likely to be active or feel like being around other people. By looking after your physical health, you can improve your mental and emotional well-being – And by looking after your mental health, you can improve your emotional and physical well-being. Do not neglect these areas of your health – If you feel that something is not right, address it and look at the options available to help you improve it. If you feel unsure about what the cause of the problem is and how to resolve it, reach out to someone for support – it could be someone you know or it could be a professional. The worst thing you can do is ignore the issue and hope it will go away, because it will creep into other areas of your life. Take the steps to make a change and do not be afraid to ask for help if you need it – we all need support sometimes.

[Mindset]

I used to think that mindset meant approaching every situation with a positive attitude, but no one can keep positive in every situation. There will be times when you feel everything but positive and happy, and that is completely fine. Mindset is about the attitude you have towards a situation and how you think about things. Before my break up, I strongly disliked big changes and would only try new things within my comfort zone. I worked to make everything in my life 'perfect', by only focusing on improving the things I knew I could be good at. I would avoid new challenges, instead working to make everything in my life as flawless as possible. When my relationship broke down, I was thrust into a whole new chapter of my life which was drastically different and presented a hill of various challenges and imperfections in my experience. It was an incredibly tough time and it took a lot for me to get used to, but as life turned around for the better, I realised that the change and the challenge allowed me to grow and learn significantly more than I had in years. The change that I was so afraid of making, became the start of a whole new, better version of myself and my life, and now I embrace positive change in every area of my life, to allow me to keep growing and learning. I know starting over is scary and you may have a lot of questions along the way, but once you are through that storm, think about how much you have grown and how much you have learnt, for the better.

[Choosing the right team players]
Be sure to spend your time with people you genuinely value and want to be a part of your life – People who bring positivity to your life, who you have a mutual respect for and have shared principles. These are the people who will understand your values, goals and desires and be supportive of what you want to achieve in life, because they are aiming for or have achieved similar things. It is said that you are an accumulation of the people you spend the most time with, so

surrounding yourself with the right people is vital. The right people will enrich your life and you will find common benefit in your relationship. When these elements are missing from a relationship, the connection can become strained and unfulfilling – one person may feel as if they contribute over and above, whilst the other person may feel undervalued or disrespected. Having the right balance is key for any relationship, whether that be friends, business partners, mentors/mentees or couples. For couples, an imbalance in values, goals and desires creates a bigger issue than other relationship types, because these are the elements which a part of the foundation for a life together. If these are not aligned for the couple, then it means they have different expectations for the relationship and are not heading in the same direction. Try to identify indifferences in your relationships as early as possible and see if they can be aligned, but do not force an alignment. Both parties have the right to live the life they choose and if by coming together, one or both have to settle then it will create problems in the longer term. You deserve to live the life you want and so does your potential partner – be realistic about what you want for your life and what you do not want.

No one else can or will walk this journey of life for you. It is your story, your experience. There will always be people there to support you as you face the challenges and celebrate the wins, but they are also all walking their own path, with their own goals and own needs.

So be careful not to get caught up in someone else's journey and ensure you take care of your needs, your wants, your health and yourself along the way.

Chapter Ten

Not the end

Synopsis: Remembering that difficult periods are not the end, just the beginning of a new chapter.

I would love to tell you that everything is perfect and works out in the end, but this is not a Disney story. Life is full of ups and downs, and will continue to be. The journey will test you in many ways: there will be times when you feel low and need a break; there will be moments of uncertainty; and there will be times when you feel massively motivated to push forward. It is your approach to the ups and downs that matters. When you come up against a big change or challenge, are you going to hide away, or take control and face up to it with the confidence of knowing, that on the other side of this hurdle is victory and personal growth.

Starting over changed my life beyond what I could have known. Whilst I knew subconsciously that I was unhappy in my relationship and the life I was living, I wrongly felt I had little other choice but to make the best of my situation and live my life going through the motions. When the connection finally broke down, instead of seeing opportunity and new possibilities, I felt like I had reached a dead end road and had nowhere else to turn. The nights that I spent hours crying into my pillow, heartbroken and feeling alone, I could never have imagined how my life would have changed and improved for the better. The breakdown of my relationship was difficult, however it was the catalyst to force me into a new path and change the life I was unhappy with. Now, I try to be more honest with myself – recognising people, situations and attitudes that are no longer right for me and adjust quickly. Additionally, I no longer fear change, because I know the outcome could improve my life in a way I may not have been able to imagine, even if there is a difficult road to walk to get there. Instead, whenever I feel a lull in my life, I actively seek to bring positive change and push pass my comfort limits.

The ending of one chapter is not the end of your story – actually, it is a fresh page for new possibilities and new direction. As you adjust to the change, take the time to think about the last chapter, considering the things that made you happy, the things you want to improve and the things you want to say goodbye to. It may be hard to see the opportunity at first, especially if the change was unexpected, but the more you evaluate and focus on what you do and do not want in your life, the more you will see what is potentially available to you in your new chapter.

"So as you step out there and begin to build lives that you know you can build, never get set back by a little bump in the road." Michelle Obama

[Take a leap of faith]
As you start over, do not be constrained by what is available to you. Dream big and go after what you want. There may be new

opportunities open to you straight away, or it may take some time and work to find and develop the opportunities available to you, however when these align with your vision, jump at them. You do not have to have everything perfectly lined up, ready and waiting to take that move – take a leap of faith, trusting that everything will work out as it is meant to be. And if it does not work out as you want, there is a lesson which will help you learn, grow, and be more prepared for the next opportunity that comes your way.

I took a leap of faith when I put an offer on a house that I barely had the deposit for, where the sellers wanted to complete the sale as quickly as possible. When my offer was accepted, I was then told by the bank that they required a bigger deposit from me because I did not have a perfect credit history. I stressed and worried about losing the opportunity, racking my brains to think about how I would scrap together enough money to complete the purchase in the short time frame that the sellers insisted on. In the end, the sale took twice as long as a normal house purchase because of the slow progress on the seller's side, giving me six more months to save every penny I had in order to get the home that I needed. The end result did not come easy and during that time, I relied strongly on faith to get me through the uncertainty, however I never would have been able to achieve that success without taking a leap of faith at the beginning, when nothing was perfectly aligned.

You will not be able to work out every detail and challenge of your journey before you take your steps forward, and it might be terrifying at times to not know how things will work out – but when things work out, despite the tears, stress and sleepless nights, you will be thankful that you took a chance and kept going. There will be failure along the way and despite what people will say, it is completely natural. It would be more unusual to do everything perfectly and not face any challenges or disappointments. There are lessons in those periods – something to help you grow and improve, ready for the next challenge or opportunity. Your story is about how you deal with failures and come back from them – that is what counts!

"It always seems impossible until it's done"
Nelson Mandela

[Live for you]
In ten years' time, when you look back on this period of your life, will you be happy about the way you lived your life? Will you feel that you made all the right choices to live the life that you wanted and in the way you wanted? Or will you be wishing you followed your heart over your head and took a chance on you? If you are not doing the things to make you feel happy and fulfilled in your life, then what are you

doing? Starting over allows you to really evaluate where you are and focus on where you want to be. If you do not know what you want, then take the time to figure it out – it is your life so you should be the driving force behind what it looks like. As I said previously, without a destination, you are going nowhere – you decide the destination and direction. They say 'You will never be as young again, as you are right now' – Live the life you want to live, in the way you want to live, to become the person you want to be.

Avoid comparing your life to other people's lives. You have your own road to walk along which you will learn and grow from, but if you keep watching what others are doing, you will steer yourself off track. It is tempting to look at other people's situation and believe they are on a better road than you, especially in the age of social media, where many people show the best versions of their life to the world. Remember the pictures and videos are just incredibly short moments within a person's life and what they show you is not always the reality of the life they are living. Everyone has struggles that they deal with: some people will be very open about their issues; whilst others may choose to only talk about their problems once they have dealt with them; or never talk about their struggles at all. You can gain knowledge and understanding from someone who has been through a similar situation or journey as you, however not everything they may have done to overcome that challenge in their life will work perfectly for you – in some aspects, you will have to find your own way. No-one has walked the road you have walked or dealt with all the things you have dealt with, so no one can tell you how to feel at any stage in your life. There may be people who can empathise and offer their experiences as suggestion – be open to the advice they have to offer, but remember your solution is tailored for you and you must do what is right for you. So take the snippets and experiences that are most relevant to you and apply it to your life as best you think.

[Remember that challenges come with growth]
When I look back on the journey I have been on, it's hard to believe how much life has evolved for the better. When you are at your lowest moments, it feels unachievable to regain even the smallest joys, but there comes a time when you look back at all you have achieved despite the difficult circumstances and you will be amazed. You will overcome the challenges, the upset, the hurt and you will learn lessons from it. Remember that on difficult days, as hard as it may be – it will improve and one day you may even be glad for it.

"One day, in retrospect, the years of struggle will strike you as the most beautiful" Sigmund Freud

Special Thanks to

Colin Tomlin

Judy Tomlin

Catherine Irwin

Toni-Ann Smith

and

Priya Tank

Printed in Great Britain
by Amazon

62421311R00088